The Spiritual Symbols Workbook

Create your personal dictionary of intuitive, psychic and metaphysical symbols

Rev. Joanna Bartlett

Alight Press

Cover images used under license from Shutterstock.com, © 2016 Romolo Tavani and tose.

Interior images © 2016 An_Vino, apokusay, Ardely, AuraStock, Chantall, Doggygraph, Drekhann, fafarumba, kostenkodesign, mIRonchik, Netkoff, theerapol, and YAZZIK. Licensed from VectorStock®.

ISBN-10: 1945489030
ISBN-13: 978-1-945489-03-7

Alight Press LLC
Eugene, OR 97405

www.alightpress.com

Printed in the United States of America

Contents

Introduction

About this workbook

Spirit often talks to you in symbols — through your dreams, through flashes of insight, through moments in your everyday life that somehow feel connected to the divine.

By knowing what different symbols mean, you can understand the messages you're being given.

While there are dictionaries that define the different symbols you might receive through dreams, intuition and psychic messages, what those symbols mean to you may not be the same as the standard definition. Symbolic meanings are personal, colored by your individual associations with that image, idea or word. The best way you can interpret the unique messages you receive is to learn what different symbols mean to you.

It's true that you can ask each and every time when you receive the message what a certain symbol means. But it's much easier and less confusing to have an established set of symbols through which Spirit can work with you. It's like psychic shorthand. Plus, the more in tune you are with your symbols, the more you'll receive messages using the ones you're most familiar with.

Every book about intuition development and psychic development that I've read, and all the classes I've taken, have instructed me to create a symbol dictionary of my own. I ask all my students to do the same and to fill it in as they meditate and work on developing their intuition and mediumship skills. But do they? Nope. It's logistically difficult. Everything ends up in a hodgepodge of jumbled symbols, no categories, no order. How do you find each entry when you need it?

The hardest part of creating your own symbol dictionary is organizing it so you can find the information again later. I've done that work for you, separating all the common symbols into different categories and organizing them alphabetically within categories. While I've included every symbol I can think of, you'll probably come up with a few more and there's room in each category for you write in your own symbols and their meanings.

About the author

I'm an ordained Spiritualist minister and certified medium through the National Spiritualist Association of Churches. I began practicing mediumship and spiritual healing in 2001 and received my ordination in 2007.

As a teacher, I've offered mediumship development classes, circles and mentorship to hundreds of students, many of whom have gone on to be successful mediums and psychics. I continue to offer classes in mediumship and intuitive development, and have authored several books on the subject including *Spirit Energy, Spirit Circle Games, Signs from Spirit Journal*, and the *Led by Light* series of books for developing intuitive mediumship abilities.

Just like my students, I'm continuing to grow and learn, and welcome your feedback on this workbook. You can contact me at www.revjoannabartlett.com.

The meaning and power of symbols

How do symbols come to you?

Symbols can come to you in all sorts of ways. Think of them as a shorthand method of communication from your inner or higher self and Spirit.

We most often think of symbols as part of our dreams — as we know that many of the things we experience in dreams are symbolic in nature rather than literal. While there are many dream dictionaries with archetypal, common definitions of dream images, your interpretations may differ.

We also receive symbols as part of our connection with our intuition. You can receive intuitive information through your dreams, but also through sudden images, sounds, smells, feelings or flashes of thought.

Another method of receiving symbolic information is through meditation. Whether you meditate for mindfulness or relaxation, or to connect with your higher self, spirit guides or your understanding of God, you'll often receive information that's symbolic in nature.

And, if you're developing your psychic or mediumship abilities, symbols are a big part of receiving messages from Spirit, spirit guides and loved ones.

In all of these methods of receiving symbolic information, you just need to know what they mean.

Why do we use symbols?

Symbols create links between different concepts and experiences. They are a constant part of our lives. Symbols are the foundation of all communication, written and verbal. Numbers and letters themselves are symbols, forming sounds. Rearranged into different, agreed-upon combinations in each language, they become words, each with its own meaning.

The meaning of a word is also more than its literal definition. The word "father" for instance means a man who has offspring. But, to you, "father" may be associated with warmth, protection and comfort, whereas to your friend it may bring up feelings of anger and punishment. Or it could feel like loss and longing if a father was absent from your childhood. It all depends on your association with the word based on your experiences with it.

These associations and how they color your personal meanings are related to your filters.

Understanding your filters

Everyone has filters. You experience the world through your own particular lens. So do I. We all do. And that's OK.

Your perception of your experiences colors your experiences, usually in the moment of having the experience. For instance, if you tend toward optimism and believing the universe is on your side, you'll tend to experience obstacles as temporary setbacks that you'll navigate your way around. If you are of a more cynical disposition, you may see setbacks as evidence that the world is out to get you.

Your filters also allow you to only see so much. Ever notice how you'll take a photo and look at it later and see details you didn't notice when you initially took it? Perhaps someone photobombed it or there are interesting shadows that your mind didn't perceive at the time. That's your mind filtering out information, giving you only the information it believes to be necessary and relevant at each moment.

The thing to remember is that filters aren't necessarily bad. Understanding what they are, where they come from and how they relate to working with Spirit will help you understand your own symbols.

Where filters come from

Your filters are based on the sum of your experiences, They're influenced by the languages you speak and the cultures you grew up in and have been exposed to. This includes the TV shows you've watched, music you've listened to and food you've eaten, as well as places you've visited, activities you've tried and books you've read.

Spirit uses the experiences you've had to communicate with you in a language you can understand.

Together, all your experiences amass a sort of internal database of things in known existence to you. You only know what you know. And you can't really know what you don't know.

What this means is that you'll see symbols that are familiar to you, especially if you are working on your own internal symbol dictionary while developing your intuition or understanding your dreams. If you're doing intuitive or psychic readings for others, then you may see things from their internal database of experiences that are unfamiliar to you, or from that of their loved one if you're practicing mediumship. However, for the most part, you're going to be working with symbols that you've encountered before, at one time or another, in some context.

Plus, the more you work with your own symbols and strengthen your connection to what they mean to you, the more Spirit will use those symbols with your interpretations during whatever work you're doing. Your own intuition, your spirit guides and Spirit itself wants you to understand and for communication to be as clear as possible. But it takes effort, by both parties. The more work you do on your end, the less energy it takes for that communication to take place and the more accurate it is.

Working with filters

This is where your own filters come into play. How your perception colored the experience you had with a particular symbol when you previously encountered it in your life is likely to affect your interpretation of that symbol now.

This is why your interpretation of a symbol might be markedly different from the traditional interpretation. For instance, the traditional symbolic interpretation of a rose is love and beauty, often romantic love. It's connected to the colors red and pink. It can also be symbolic of keeping secrets.

For me, roses symbolize love and are strongly connected to my mother, who loved roses.

However, if you were a fictional character in a best-selling book and movie trilogy whose nemesis used the fragrance of roses to cover up the smell of poison, roses might mean something different. They might mean death and betrayal, lies and deceit. (I'm referencing Katniss in Suzanne Collins' *The Hunger Games*, here.)

Again, the more you strengthen your understanding of symbols and work with what they mean to you, the more you'll receive those symbols as your interpretation of them (even if they're coming from another person in physical or etheric form).

If you receive a symbol and what it initially brings up for you doesn't quite feel right, e.g. I see or smell a rose, but somehow it doesn't feel like it's connected to my mother, then go deeper and ask for more information and clarity. Perhaps this time the rose is about keeping secrets. Or that you need to look more closely or carefully at something to be aware of the hidden thorns beneath the beauty. Trust your intuition.

Your symbol interpretations can deepen over time, the more you work with them. So feel free to update this workbook as you continue your intuitive journey.

Expanding your internal database

If you can only understand symbols that are already in your database, that you've previously encountered in your life, does that mean you're limited to only those symbols? Not necessarily.

You can expand your database. You do this by being open to new experiences and continuing to explore cultures, activities, languages, foods and drinks — everything your senses can pick up. If you're drawn to a particular culture, religion or activity, learn more about it. You may be surprised how quickly you'll start receiving symbols that are related to it. I've even been known to get messages related to whatever silly game I've been playing most recently on my cell phone.

Try new foods, explore new places, participate in a new sport, hobby or group activity. Go out and experience the world. It all feeds your symbol database, giving you more experiences to drawn upon and enabling greater and better communication with Spirit and your own divine self.

How this workbook is organized

The workbook is separated into several (hopefully) logical categories. Categories are organized alphabetically. Subcategories and items within each category and subcategory are also organized alphabetically.

Putting all the most likely symbols into categories was a complicated task. What makes sense to me, may not intuitively make sense to you. If so, I'm sorry about that. There's also an index in the back if my organizational system flummoxes you.

Here are the categories and what each of them cover:

Animals (organized by phylum and/or class)

- Amphibians
- Birds
- Fish
- Insects
- Invertebrates
- Mammals
- Reptiles

Body (the parts of your body, heat, feet, etc.)

Colors

Food

- Condiments
- Dairy
- Drinks
- Fats and oils
- Fruits
- Grains, beans and legumes
- Meat
- Sweets
- Vegetables

House (things you usually find inside or outside a house)

- General
- Appliances
- Areas of the house

- Doors
- Furniture
- Outside

Nature

- General
- Cosmic
- Directions
- Elements
- Flowers
- Gems and minerals
- Metals
- Places
- Planets
- Plants
- Seasons
- Times of Day
- Trees
- Weather

Numbers

- Numbers 1-20
- Repeated numbers

Objects

- Everyday
- Instruments
- Tools
- Toys and games

People (all things related to the things people do, wear, work, etc.)

- General
- Activities
- Clothing and accessories
- Events
- Mythical
- Professions

Places (not already covered in Nature - Places)

- General
- Geographical areas
- Landmarks

Religious symbols (everything I could think of from many of the major religions and some lesser known ones as well)

Shapes

Tarot cards

- Major arcana cards
- Minor arcana cards

Traffic signs

Vehicles and transportation

Zodiac signs

Things to keep in mind

If you don't know what some of the items are in a category, that's OK. It's all about what's in your specific database based on your personal experience.

People who love dogs know all the dog breeds. It's the same with people who love birds or who have studied the major religions. If you don't know anything about birds, you might only get the basics of the bird: its color, for instance, or only the birds you are familiar with.

You may also be surprised that you can see a symbol and intuitively know what kind of animal, tree, flower or symbol it is, even though you don't know how you know it.

Conversely, if you're an expert in a particular area, there are probably symbols I've left out, because they're not well-known or common symbols. This is especially true for animal and plant species. For that purpose, there's space on each page for you add additional items.

I also welcome your feedback on what I should include in future editions of this workbook or how it can be better organized. You can reach me at www.eugenemedium.com.

Filling out your own definitions

There's no one right way to develop your symbol dictionary. Figure out what works best for your own nature and go with it. A huge part of this process is trusting yourself, so trust how you feel moved to interact with this workbook. I've outlined a couple of ways of using this book below. You may come up with your own — that's OK, too.

Also keep in mind that your symbols can change over time. So if your personal meaning shifts and deepens as you continue this journey, that's OK. Trust yourself.

The methodical method

One by one, from start to finish

One way to figure out your meanings for different symbols is to consciously and deliberately go through each category, while in a meditative state, and write down what you get for each symbol.

Pick a category and go through each item in turn. Meditate on the item or ask your intuition what it means to you. Jot down whatever first comes to mind.

If you don't get anything for a symbol, skip over it and go to the next item on the page that you do get something for.

This is a thorough and conscientious approach. If it appeals to you, go for it.

The in-the-moment method

As they come up

As symbols come up in meditations, dreams or throughout the day, ask what they mean. Allow yourself to get quiet inside, tap into your inner guidance and wisdom and write down whatever comes up for that specific symbol.

Over time, you'll fill in definitions and information for the symbols that occur most often for you.

Inspiration through coloring

I've included several coloring pages within this book at the beginning of each category as starting off points for you. Coloring can be a form of meditation. As you color the symbols in the coloring pages, allow your mind to relax and open and let the meaning of the symbol float into your awareness. While it wasn't practical to have a coloring image for each symbol in this workbook, they are meant as a starting point to access your imagination and intuition.

If meditative coloring works well for you to connect with your intuition, I encourage you to continue to use coloring books to access your inner wisdom. *Intuitive Symbols Coloring Book: Unlock your intuition through meditative coloring* is meant as a companion book to this workbook. And there are plenty of other adult coloring books, on a variety of themes, available online and in bookstores.

Use all your senses

No matter how you fill out your definitions in this workbook, when you connect in with the meaning of each symbol, use all of your senses. If you're writing about the symbolic meaning of an apple, see the apple in your mind's eye, smell it, taste it, hear the crunch as you bite into it, feel the resistance of the peel against your teeth. Are there memories or emotions connected to this symbol? Does it bring you sudden knowing or insight?

We often think of symbols as visual things, but all of our senses are part of our internal database. Scents, in particular, are strongly associated with memory and emotion. Use that to your advantage and use all of your physical senses to access your intuition.

Trust yourself

Trust what comes up for you for each symbol. A specific symbol doesn't have to mean the same to you as it does to anyone else, especially if you're doing this work to develop your own intuition and connection with your higher self, Spirit or your spirit guides or to understand your dreams.

If you initially get nothing or something that doesn't quite feel right, go deeper within yourself. The still, quiet place within you is a source of tremendous knowledge. All the answers you need are there for you.

Meditation methods

Meditation is a wonderful thing. It has a host of scientifically-proven health benefits, including lowering your blood pressure, increasing your immunity and allowing you to concentrate better. Developing a regular meditation habit is highly recommended.

You can start with a couple of minutes a day, wherever it fits into your schedule — in the morning when you first wake up, right before you go to sleep at night or anywhere in between.

You might find you meditate well while folding laundry, washing dishes or doing other routine tasks (this is called active meditation).

Or you may prefer to intentionally give yourself a few minutes to breathe deeply, calming your mind and body, clearing and focusing your thoughts (this is mental meditation).

You can meditate anywhere, although for mental meditation you'll probably prefer to be somewhere private where you won't be interrupted.

Below are some meditation methods I like to use and which I teach to my students. You can use gentle, uplifting music during these meditations, or do them in silence. Try different meditation music and no music at all and see what works best for you.

The purpose of these meditation techniques is to teach you how to enter into a calm, quiet state of mind, stilling your mental chatter. By doing so, you'll be able to access your inner wisdom and intuition.

Mindfulness meditation

The goal of mindfulness meditation is to help you focus on the now and live in each present moment. By becoming more present with yourself, as you are right now, you're able to participate more fully in each moment of your life. It can also help you learn to focus your mind as you gently bring it back (over and over and over again) to the present moment each time it wanders off.

An important thing to know about mindfulness meditation is that its goal isn't that you'll stop thinking or be able to sit with an empty mind. Its point is for you to learn to notice what is at the focus of your attention and to be able to move that point of focus, without judgment, to what you want it to be (in this case, your breath). Mindfulness is about accepting yourself where you are in each present moment.

Within mindfulness meditation, there are a range of techniques. You can meditate with your eyes open or closed, for instance. Try out different things and find out what works best for you (I like to close my eyes).

Here's one technique:

- To start, take 3 deep breaths, in through your nose and out through your mouth. Let go of everything that brought you to where you are and just be in the present moment.
- Relax your breath, breathing into and out of your nose. Don't force it, just let it be.
- Bring your awareness and attention to your breath, without changing how you're breathing.
- Notice how your breath enters your body and how it leaves it.
- Notice how it feels at the first moment of your inhalation, the fullness of your inhalation, the first

moment of your exhalation and at the end of your exhale.

- As your mind wanders, gently bring it back to your body and your breath.

- As thoughts come into your mind (which they will do, it's just the way of thoughts), bring your attention back to your breath. Release any judgment you have of yourself for having thoughts. They're OK and natural. Just notice that you've been thinking and move your attention back to your breath.

Breathing meditation

This is similar to mindfulness meditation in that it focuses on the breath. But it does so with some simple techniques to help your mind focus more easily. These methods are helpful if you want to find moments of mental stillness during meditation but have difficulty with your mind constantly wandering away or feeling anxious.

I often use these methods (especially the first one) if I'm having trouble falling asleep when my mind keeps whirring trying to solve all of my problems and those of the world in the middle of the night.

Method 1: inhale/exhale

- As you inhale, mentally say to yourself, "inhale."

- As you exhale, mentally say to yourself, "exhale."

- Repeat.

An alternative to this technique is to say to yourself "Now I am inhaling" as you inhale and "Now I am exhaling" as you exhale.

Method 2: count to 10

- As you inhale, mentally count, "1."

- As you exhale, mentally count, "2."

- Continue going: inhale "3," exhale "4," inhale "5," exhale "6," inhale "7," exhale "8," inhale "9," exhale "10."

- Then start again from 1 and repeat.

Open meditation

As you regularly practice the meditation techniques above, you'll become more adept at reaching a meditative state quickly and easily. At some point, you'll be able to close your eyes, take some slow, full breaths and set your intention to meditate and you'll be in that calm, quiet place inside yourself.

Once you're in that place, you can ask your inner self, spirit guides or your understanding of God for guidance and answers.

If you're following the methodical method, you can open your workbook and go through each category and symbol in turn.

If you're in the in-the-moment crowd, you can go into the meditation with a specific question or situation in mind, asking for clarity and understanding. As information comes up in the form of symbols, ask what it means. Ask if your immediate thought or feeling about the symbol is its true meaning for you, or if you need to go deeper beneath the surface. Trust what comes. And write it down in your workbook.

Animals

Animals - Amphibians

Alligator

_____

_____

_____

Bull frog

_____

_____

_____

Frog

_____

_____

_____

Newt

_____

_____

_____

Salamander

_____

_____

_____

Toad

_____

_____

_____

_____

_____

_____

_____

_____

_____

_____

Animals - Birds

Albatross

Black swan

Blackbird

Blue jay

Budgie

Buzzard

Canary

Cardinal

Chick

Chickadee

_____

_____

_____

Chicken

_____

_____

_____

Condor

_____

_____

_____

Cormorant

_____

_____

_____

Crane

_____

_____

_____

Crow

_____

_____

_____

Cuckoo

_____

_____

_____

Dodo bird

_____

_____

_____

Dove

_____

_____

_____

_____

Duck

_____

_____

_____

Eagle

_____

_____

_____

Egret

_____

_____

_____

Emu

_____

_____

_____

Falcon

_____

_____

_____

Finch

_____

_____

_____

Flamingo

_____

_____

_____

Goose

_____

_____

_____

Grouse

_____

_____

_____

_____

_____

Gull

_____

_____

_____

Hawk

_____

_____

_____

Hen

_____

_____

_____

Heron

_____

_____

_____

Hummingbird

_____

_____

_____

Kingfisher

_____

_____

_____

Kookaburra

_____

_____

_____

Loon

_____

_____

_____

Macaw

_____

_____

_____

_____

_____

Animals - Birds

Magpie

Meadowlark

Mockingbird

Nighthawk

Nightingale

Osprey

Ostrich

Owl

Parakeet

20

Parrot

_____

_____

Partridge

_____

_____

Peacock

_____

_____

Pelican

_____

_____

Pheasant

_____

_____

Pigeon

_____

_____

Quail

_____

_____

Raven

_____

_____

Red-tailed hawk

_____

_____

_____

_____

Robin

_____

_____

_____

Rooster

_____

_____

Sandpiper

_____

_____

Seagull

_____

_____

Shrew

_____

_____

Sidewinder

_____

_____

Snow goose

_____

_____

Sparrow

_____

_____

Starling

_____

_____

_____

_____

Stork

_____

_____

_____

Swan

_____

_____

_____

Turkey

_____

_____

_____

Vulture

_____

_____

_____

Woodpecker

_____

_____

_____

Wren

_____

_____

_____

_____

_____

_____

_____

_____

_____

_____

_____

_____

Angelfish

_____

_____

_____

Barracuda

_____

_____

_____

Bass

_____

_____

_____

Beta

_____

_____

_____

Bluefish

_____

_____

_____

Catfish

_____

_____

_____

Clownfish

_____

_____

_____

Cod

_____

_____

_____

Dory

_____

_____

_____

Animals - Fish

Eel

_____

_____

_____

Flying fish

_____

_____

_____

Goldfish

_____

_____

_____

Guppy

_____

_____

_____

Halibut

_____

_____

_____

Koi

_____

_____

_____

Platy

_____

_____

_____

Ray

_____

_____

_____

Salmon

_____

_____

_____

_____

_____

Sea horse

_____
_____
_____

Shark

_____
_____
_____

Skate

_____
_____
_____

Snapper

_____
_____
_____

Stingray

_____
_____
_____

Tetra

_____
_____
_____

Trout

_____
_____
_____

Tuna

_____
_____
_____
_____
_____
_____
_____

Ant

_____

_____

_____

Bee

_____

_____

_____

Beetle

_____

_____

_____

Bug

_____

_____

_____

Bumblebee

_____

_____

_____

Butterfly

_____

_____

_____

Caterpillar

_____

_____

_____

Cicada

_____

_____

_____

Cockroach

_____

_____

_____

Cricket

Dragonfly

Dung beetle

Firefly

Flea

Fly

Grasshopper

Honey bee

Hornet

Katydid

Ladybug

Lightning bug

Locust

Maggot

Mosquito

Moth

Praying mantis

Spider web

Wasp

Centipede

_____
_____
_____

Clam

_____
_____
_____

Coral

_____
_____
_____

Crab

_____
_____
_____

Crustacean

_____
_____
_____

Earthworm

_____
_____
_____

Horseshoe crab

_____
_____
_____

Hydra

_____
_____
_____

Inch worm

_____
_____
_____

Insects

Jellyfish

Leech

Lobster

Millipede

Mite

Octopus

Oyster

Scorpion

Sea anemone

Sea cucumber

Sea urchin

Slug

Snail

Spider

Squid

Starfish

Tarantula

Urchin

Worm

Animals - Mammals

Aardvark

Alpaca

Anteater

Antelope

Ape

Armadillo

Baboon

Badger

Bat

Beagle

_____

_____

_____

Bear

_____

_____

_____

Beaver

_____

_____

_____

Bison

_____

_____

_____

Bloodhound

_____

_____

_____

Boar

_____

_____

_____

Bobcat

_____

_____

_____

Boxer dog

_____

_____

_____

Buffalo

_____

_____

_____

_____

Bull

_____
_____
_____

Bulldog

_____
_____
_____

Camel

_____
_____
_____

Caribou

_____
_____
_____

Cat

_____
_____
_____

Cheetah

_____
_____
_____

Chihuahua

_____
_____
_____

Chimpanzee

_____
_____
_____

Chipmunk

_____
_____
_____
_____
_____

Cocker spaniel

Collie

Cougar

Cow

Coyote

Dachshund

Deer

Dingo

Doberman

Dog

_____

_____

_____

Dolphin

_____

_____

_____

Donkey

_____

_____

_____

Elephant

_____

_____

_____

Elk

_____

_____

_____

Ferret

_____

_____

_____

Fox

_____

_____

_____

Gazelle

_____

_____

_____

Gerbil

_____

_____

_____

_____

_____

German shepherd

Giraffe

Goat

Golden retriever

Gopher

Gorilla

Great Dane

Grizzly bear

Groundhog

Guinea pig

_____

_____

_____

Hare

_____

_____

_____

Hedgehog

_____

_____

_____

Hippopotamus

_____

_____

_____

Horse

_____

_____

_____

Hyena

_____

_____

_____

Impala

_____

_____

_____

Jackal

_____

_____

_____

Jackrabbit

_____

_____

_____

_____

Jaguar

_____

_____

_____

Kangaroo

_____

_____

_____

Killer whale

_____

_____

_____

Kitten

_____

_____

_____

Koala

_____

_____

_____

Labrador retriever

_____

_____

_____

Lamb

_____

_____

_____

Lemming

_____

_____

_____

Leopard

_____

_____

_____

_____

Lion

Llama

Lynx

Manatee

Marmot

Meerkat

Mice

Miniature schnauzer

Mole

Mongoose

_____
_____

Monkey

_____
_____

Moose

_____
_____

Mountain lion

_____
_____

Mouse

_____
_____

Mule

_____
_____

Musk ox

_____
_____

Narwhal

_____
_____

Ocelot

_____
_____
_____
_____

Orangutan

Orca

Otter

Ox

Panda

Panther

Penguin

Pig

Platypus

Polar bear

_____

_____

_____

Pomeranian

_____

_____

_____

Pony

_____

_____

_____

Poodle

_____

_____

_____

Porcupine

_____

_____

_____

Possum

_____

_____

_____

Prairie dog

_____

_____

_____

Puffin

_____

_____

_____

Pug

_____

_____

_____

_____

Puma

_____

_____

_____

Rabbit

_____

_____

_____

Raccoon

_____

_____

_____

Ram

_____

_____

_____

Rat

_____

_____

_____

Reindeer

_____

_____

_____

Rhinoceros

_____

_____

_____

Roadrunner

_____

_____

_____

Rottweiler

_____

_____

_____

_____

_____

Saint Bernard

Schnauzer

Sea lion

Seal

Sheep

Sheepdog

Shih tzu

Siberian husky

Skunk

Sloth

_____

_____

_____

Squirrel

_____

_____

_____

Tiger

_____

_____

_____

Whale

_____

_____

_____

Wildebeest

_____

_____

_____

Wolf

_____

_____

_____

Woodchuck

_____

_____

_____

Yak

_____

_____

_____

Yorkshire terrier

_____

_____

_____

_____

Zebra

Basilisk

Centaur

Chimera

Dragon

Fairy

Ghoul

Gnome

Griffin

Hippogriff

Loch Ness monster

Mermaid

Merman

Pegasus

Pixie

Sphinx

Troll

Unicorn

Werewolf

Yeti

Animals - Mythical

Anaconda

Chameleon

Crocodile

Dinosaur

Gecko

Iguana

Komodo dragon

Lizard

Python

Rattlesnake

Scorpion

Snake

Tortoise

Turtle

Body

Ankle

_____

_____

_____

Arm

_____

_____

_____

Back

_____

_____

_____

Bald head

_____

_____

_____

Beard

_____

_____

_____

Blood

_____

_____

_____

Bones

_____

_____

_____

Bottom

_____

_____

_____

Brain

_____

_____

_____

_____

Body

Breasts

_____

_____

_____

Ear(s)

_____

_____

_____

Eye(s)

_____

_____

_____

Face

_____

_____

_____

Finger(s)

_____

_____

_____

Fist

_____

_____

_____

Foot

_____

_____

_____

Forehead

_____

_____

_____

Hair

_____

_____

_____

_____

_____

Hand

_____
_____
_____

Head

_____
_____
_____

Heart

_____
_____
_____

Heel

_____
_____
_____

Hips

_____
_____
_____

Jaw

_____
_____
_____

Knee

_____
_____
_____

Labia

_____
_____
_____

Leg

_____
_____
_____
_____
_____

Body

Lips

Lungs

Mouth

Neck

Nose

Ovaries

Pelvis

Penis

Scrotum

Shin

Shoulder

Stomach

Tear

Teeth

Thigh

Throat

Toes

Tongue

Body

Vagina

_____

_____

_____

Wings

_____

_____

_____

Womb

_____

_____

_____

_____

_____

_____

_____

_____

_____

_____

_____

_____

_____

_____

_____

_____

_____

_____

_____

_____

_____

_____

_____

Colors

Amber

_____

_____

_____

Aquamarine

_____

_____

_____

Black

_____

_____

_____

Blue

_____

_____

_____

Brown

_____

_____

_____

Fuchsia

_____

_____

_____

Gold

_____

_____

_____

Green

_____

_____

_____

Grey

_____

_____

_____

Indigo

_____

_____

_____

Ivory

_____

_____

_____

Magenta

_____

_____

_____

Maroon

_____

_____

_____

Orange

_____

_____

_____

Pink

_____

_____

_____

Purple

_____

_____

_____

Red

_____

_____

_____

Silver

_____

_____

_____

_____

_____

Colors

Tan

_____

_____

_____

Violet

_____

_____

_____

White

_____

_____

_____

Yellow

_____

_____

_____

_____

_____

_____

_____

_____

_____

_____

_____

_____

_____

_____

_____

_____

_____

_____

_____

_____

_____

Food

Hot sauce

_____

_____

_____

Ketchup

_____

_____

_____

Mayonnaise

_____

_____

_____

Mustard

_____

_____

_____

Salad dressing

_____

_____

_____

Steak sauce

_____

_____

_____

Vanilla

_____

_____

_____

Vinegar

_____

_____

_____

_____

_____

_____

Butter

_____
_____
_____

Cheese

_____
_____
_____

Chocolate milk

_____
_____
_____

Cottage cheese

_____
_____
_____

Cream

_____
_____
_____

Cream cheese

_____
_____
_____

Custard

_____
_____
_____

Hard cheese

_____
_____
_____

Ice cream

_____
_____
_____

Milk

Soft cheese

Sour cream

Yogurt

Food - Drinks

Alcohol

_____
_____
_____

Beer

_____
_____
_____

Champagne

_____
_____
_____

Cider

_____
_____
_____

Coffee

_____
_____
_____

Energy drink

_____
_____
_____

Fruit juice

_____
_____
_____

Hard cider

_____
_____
_____

Soda

_____
_____
_____

Tea

Vegetable juice

Water

Wine

Food - Drinks

Lard

Oil

Olive oil

Food – Fruits

Apple

Banana

Berries

Blackberry

Coconut

Dried fruit

Fig

Fruit

Grape

Lemon
_____
_____
_____

Lime
_____
_____
_____

Mango
_____
_____
_____

Orange
_____
_____
_____

Peach
_____
_____
_____

Pear
_____
_____
_____

Pineapple
_____
_____
_____

Plum
_____
_____
_____

Prune
_____
_____
_____
_____
_____

Food - Fruits

Raspberry

Strawberry

Watermelon

Food - Grains, beans and legumes

Almonds

Amaranth

Bagel

Bread

Cashews

Cereal

Chickpeas

Corn

Corn chips

Food - Grains, beans and legumes

Cornflakes

Crepes

Crumbs

Doughnuts

Egg noodles

English muffin

Flat bread

Grain

Granola

Hot dog roll

Lentils

Macaroni

Nuts

Oatmeal

Oats

Pancakes

Pasta

Peanuts

Food - Grains, beans and legumes

Pizza

Quinoa

Rice

Rolls

Rye

Sandwich

Scones

Sliced bread

Soy

Spaghetti

_____

_____

_____

Split pea

_____

_____

_____

Sunflower seeds

_____

_____

_____

Sushi

_____

_____

_____

Taco

_____

_____

_____

Tortilla

_____

_____

_____

Waffles

_____

_____

_____

Wheat

_____

_____

_____

_____

_____

_____

_____

Food - Grains, beans and legumes

Bacon

_____

_____

_____

Beef

_____

_____

_____

Burger

_____

_____

_____

Chicken

_____

_____

_____

Chicken nuggets

_____

_____

_____

Deli meat

_____

_____

_____

Egg

_____

_____

_____

Fish

_____

_____

_____

Fish fingers

_____

_____

_____

Food - Meat

Ham

_____

_____

_____

Hot dog

_____

_____

_____

Lamb

_____

_____

_____

Meatballs

_____

_____

_____

Oysters

_____

_____

_____

Pork

_____

_____

_____

Salmon

_____

_____

_____

Sausages

_____

_____

_____

Scallops

_____

_____

_____

_____

_____

Turkey

Veal

Venison

Food - Meat

Birthday cake

_____

_____

_____

Cake

_____

_____

_____

Candy

_____

_____

_____

Chocolate

_____

_____

_____

Cookies

_____

_____

_____

Cupcake

_____

_____

_____

Danish pastry

_____

_____

_____

Icing

_____

_____

_____

Jam

_____

_____

_____

Food - Sweets

Jell-O

_____

_____

_____

Muffin

_____

_____

_____

Pie

_____

_____

_____

Plum pudding

_____

_____

_____

Popsicle

_____

_____

_____

_____

_____

_____

_____

_____

_____

_____

_____

_____

_____

_____

_____

_____

_____

Food - Vegetables

Artichoke

Basil

Beans

Bell pepper

Broccoli

Brussels sprouts

Cabbage

Carrot

Chard

Garlic

_____
_____
_____

Gourd

_____
_____
_____

Herbs

_____
_____
_____

Hot pepper

_____
_____
_____

Kale

_____
_____
_____

Leek

_____
_____
_____

Lettuce

_____
_____
_____

Mushrooms

_____
_____
_____

Onion

_____
_____
_____
_____
_____

Parsley

Peas

Potato

Pumpkin

Salad

Seaweed

Snap pea

Spinach

Sprouts

Squash

Sweetcorn

Thyme

Tomato

Vegetables

Zucchini

House

Ceiling

Electrical plug

Faucet

Fuse

Heater

Pipe

Plumbing

Toilet

Windows

House - Appliances

Air conditioner
_____
_____
_____

Furnace
_____
_____
_____

Oven
_____
_____
_____

Refrigerator
_____
_____
_____

Sink
_____
_____

Stove
_____
_____

Television
_____
_____

Washing machine
_____
_____
_____
_____
_____
_____

House - Areas

Attic

_____

_____

Balcony

_____

_____

Basement

_____

_____

Bathroom

_____

_____

Bedroom

_____

_____

Closet

_____

_____

Deck/balcony

_____

_____

Dining room

_____

_____

Family/living room

_____

_____

Fireplace
_____
_____
_____

Kitchen
_____
_____

Living room
_____
_____

Porch
_____
_____

Roof
_____
_____

Shed
_____
_____

Shower
_____
_____

Stairs
_____
_____

Threshold
_____
_____
_____
_____

House - Areas

Back door

Closed door

Front door

Locked door

Open door

Screen door

Trap door

House - Furniture

Bath

_____

_____

_____

Bed

_____

_____

_____

Blinds/curtains

_____

_____

_____

Carpet

_____

_____

_____

Chair

_____

_____

_____

Cradle/crib

_____

_____

_____

Desk

_____

_____

_____

Drawer

_____

_____

_____

Highchair

_____

_____

_____

Lamp

_____

_____

_____

Mattress

_____

_____

_____

Mirror

_____

_____

_____

Picture frame

_____

_____

_____

Seat cushion

_____

_____

_____

Sofa

_____

_____

_____

Table

_____

_____

_____

_____

_____

_____

_____

_____

_____

Arbor
_____
_____
_____

Clothesline
_____
_____
_____

Driveway
_____
_____
_____

Fence
_____
_____
_____

Garden
_____
_____
_____

Gate
_____
_____
_____

Greenhouse
_____
_____
_____

Hammock
_____
_____
_____

Hedge
_____
_____
_____

House - Outside

Hose

_____
_____
_____

Pool

_____
_____

Yard

_____
_____
_____
_____
_____
_____
_____
_____
_____
_____
_____
_____
_____
_____
_____
_____
_____
_____
_____
_____

Nature

Branch

_____

_____

_____

Bud

_____

_____

_____

Cloud

_____

_____

_____

Dirt/soil

_____

_____

_____

Feather

_____

_____

_____

Flame

_____

_____

_____

Grass

_____

_____

_____

Hay

_____

_____

_____

Landslide/avalanche

_____

_____

_____

Leaf/leaves

_____

_____

_____

Log

_____

_____

_____

Lumber/wood

_____

_____

_____

Mud

_____

_____

Nest

_____

_____

Rock

_____

_____

Sand

_____

_____

Shadow

_____

_____

Smoke

_____

_____

Stone

_____

_____

Tree

_____

_____

_____

_____

Waterfall

_____

_____

_____

Wave

_____

_____

_____

Whirlpool

_____

_____

_____

_____

_____

_____

_____

_____

_____

_____

_____

_____

_____

_____

_____

_____

_____

_____

_____

_____

_____

_____

_____

_____

_____

_____

Nature - Cosmic

(See also Nature - Planets)

Asteroid

_____

_____

_____

Comet

_____

_____

_____

Galaxy

_____

_____

_____

Meteor

_____

_____

_____

Moon

_____

_____

_____

Planet

_____

_____

_____

Star(s)

_____

_____

_____

Sun

_____

_____

_____

_____

_____

_____

East

Left

North

Right

South

West

Nature - Elements

Air

Earth

Fire

Water

Calla lily

_____
_____
_____

Carnation

_____
_____
_____

Chrysanthemum

_____
_____
_____

Daffodil

_____
_____
_____

Daisy

_____
_____
_____

Dandelion

_____
_____
_____

Flowering plant

_____
_____
_____

Forget-me-not

_____
_____
_____

Iris

_____
_____
_____

Jasmine

Lavender

Lilac

Lily

Marigold

Morning glory

Pansy

Poppy

Rose

Sunflower

_____
_____
_____

Tulip

_____
_____
_____

Violet

_____
_____
_____

Wildflowers

_____
_____
_____
_____
_____
_____
_____
_____
_____
_____
_____
_____
_____
_____
_____
_____
_____
_____
_____
_____
_____

Nature - Gems and minerals

Agate

_____

_____

_____

Alexandrite

_____

_____

_____

Amazonite

_____

_____

_____

Amber

_____

_____

_____

Amethyst

_____

_____

_____

Apatite

_____

_____

_____

Aquamarine

_____

_____

_____

Azurite

_____

_____

_____

Bloodstone

_____

_____

_____

Calcite
_____
_____
_____

Carnelian
_____
_____
_____

Coral
_____
_____
_____

Crystal
_____
_____
_____

Diamond
_____
_____
_____

Emerald
_____
_____
_____

Fluorite
_____
_____
_____

Fossil
_____
_____
_____

Garnet
_____
_____
_____
_____
_____

Gemstones
_____
_____
_____

Hematite
_____
_____

Iolite
_____
_____

Ivory
_____
_____

Jade
_____
_____

Jasper
_____
_____

Jet
_____
_____

Kyanite
_____
_____

Lapis lazuli
_____
_____
_____
_____

Nature - Gems and minerals

Lemurian seed crystals
_____
_____
_____

Malachite
_____
_____
_____

Meteorite
_____
_____
_____

Moonstone
_____
_____
_____

Obsidian
_____
_____
_____

Onyx
_____
_____
_____

Opal
_____
_____
_____

Pearl(s)
_____
_____
_____

Peridot
_____
_____
_____
_____
_____

Pyrite

_____

_____

_____

Quartz

_____

_____

_____

Rose quartz

_____

_____

_____

Ruby

_____

_____

_____

Sapphire

_____

_____

_____

Selenite

_____

_____

_____

Smoky quartz

_____

_____

_____

Sunstone

_____

_____

_____

Tiger's eye

_____

_____

_____

_____

Topaz

Tourmaline

Turquoise

Aluminum

_____

_____

_____

Brass

_____

_____

_____

Bronze

_____

_____

_____

Copper

_____

_____

_____

Gold

_____

_____

_____

Iron

_____

_____

_____

Nickel

_____

_____

_____

Platinum

_____

_____

_____

Silver

_____

_____

_____

Steel

Titanium

Abyss
_____
_____
_____

Beach
_____
_____
_____

Cliff
_____
_____
_____

Desert
_____
_____
_____

Forest
_____
_____
_____

Hill
_____
_____
_____

Island
_____
_____
_____

Lake
_____
_____
_____

Lawn
_____
_____
_____

Meadow

_____
_____
_____

Mountain

_____
_____
_____

Ocean

_____
_____
_____

Pond

_____
_____
_____

River

_____
_____
_____

Valley

_____
_____
_____

Woods

_____
_____
_____
_____
_____
_____
_____
_____
_____
_____

Earth

Jupiter

Mars

Mercury

Neptune

Pluto

Saturn

Uranus

Venus

Nature - Plants

Aloe

_____

_____

_____

Bamboo

_____

_____

_____

Banana

_____

_____

_____

Bush

_____

_____

_____

Cactus

_____

_____

_____

Four-leaf clover

_____

_____

_____

Grass

_____

_____

_____

Hemp

_____

_____

_____

Ivy

_____

_____

_____

Leaves

Passion fruit

Peanut

Peppermint

Pineapple

Plant

Poison ivy

Thistle

Thorn

Nature - Plants

Tumbleweed

_____

_____

_____

Weeds

_____

_____

_____

_____

_____

_____

_____

_____

_____

_____

_____

_____

_____

_____

_____

_____

_____

_____

_____

_____

_____

_____

_____

_____

_____

Nature - Seasons

Autumnal equinox/Mabon

_____
_____
_____

Halloween/Samhain

_____
_____
_____

Imbolc

_____
_____
_____

Lammas

_____
_____
_____

May Day/Beltane

_____
_____
_____

Spring

_____
_____
_____

Summer

_____
_____
_____

Summer solstice/Litha

_____
_____
_____

Vernal equinox/Ostara

_____
_____
_____

Winter

Winter solstice/Yule

Nature - Times of day

Dawn

_____

_____

_____

Dusk

_____

_____

_____

Night

_____

_____

_____

Noon

_____

_____

_____

Sunrise

_____

_____

_____

Sunset

_____

_____

_____

_____

_____

_____

_____

_____

_____

_____

_____

Acorn

_____

_____

Apple

_____

_____

Ash

_____

_____

Avocado

_____

_____

Beech

_____

_____

Birch

_____

_____

Bonsai

_____

_____

Cherry

_____

_____

Cymbals

_____

_____

_____

Date

Dogwood

Elder

Elm

Eucalyptus

Evergreen

Fig

Fir

Fruit

Hazel

_____

Heather

_____

Holly

_____

Japanese maple

_____

Joshua

_____

Juniper

_____

Lemon

_____

Limb

_____

Lime

_____

Nature - Trees

Magnolia

Maple

Myrtle

Nutmeg

Oak

Olive

Orange

Orchard

Palm

Peach

_____
_____
_____

Pear

_____
_____
_____

Pecan

_____
_____
_____

Pine

_____
_____
_____

Plum

_____
_____
_____

Pomegranate

_____
_____
_____

Redwood

_____
_____
_____

Sequoia

_____
_____

Walnut

_____
_____
_____
_____

Willow

Wisteria

Yew

Yucca

Nature - Weather

Blizzard

_____

_____

_____

Flood

_____

_____

_____

Fog

_____

_____

_____

Ice

_____

_____

_____

Lightning bolt

_____

_____

_____

Rain

_____

_____

_____

Rainbow

_____

_____

_____

Snow

_____

_____

_____

Storm

_____

_____

_____

Sunshine

_____

_____

_____

Thunder

_____

_____

_____

Tsunami

_____

_____

_____

Wind

_____

_____

_____

_____

_____

_____

_____

_____

_____

_____

_____

_____

_____

_____

_____

_____

_____

_____

_____

_____

_____

_____

Numbers

1, One _____

_____

_____

_____

Numbers

2, Two

_____
_____
_____

3, Three

_____
_____

4, Four

_____
_____

5, Five

_____
_____

6, Six

_____
_____

7, Seven

_____
_____

8, Eight

_____
_____

9, Nine

_____
_____

10, Ten

_____
_____
_____
_____

11, Eleven

_____

_____

12, Twelve

_____

_____

13, Thirteen

_____

_____

14, Fourteen

_____

_____

15, Fifteen

_____

_____

16, Sixteen

_____

_____

17, Seventeen

_____

_____

18, Eighteen

_____

_____

19, Nineteen

_____

_____

_____

_____

Numbers

20, Twenty

10:01

10:10

111

11:11

123

222

22:22

333

Numbers - Repeated Numbers

444

555

666

777

888

999

Objects

Alarm clock
_____
_____
_____

Antenna
_____
_____
_____

Ashes
_____
_____
_____

Bandage
_____
_____
_____

Battery
_____
_____
_____

Beads
_____
_____
_____

Bell
_____
_____
_____

Blanket
_____
_____
_____

Blindfold
_____
_____
_____

Book

_____

_____

_____

Bottle

_____

_____

_____

Box

_____

_____

_____

Brick

_____

_____

_____

Broom

_____

_____

_____

Bubble

_____

_____

_____

Business card

_____

_____

_____

Cage

_____

_____

_____

Calendar

_____

_____

_____

_____

_____

Candle

Candle holder

Casket

Cigarette

Coin

CD/DVD

Cell phone

Computer

Cup

Diary

_____

_____

_____

Diploma

_____

_____

_____

Dish

_____

_____

_____

Dollar bill

_____

_____

_____

Envelope

_____

_____

_____

Fan

_____

_____

_____

Files

_____

_____

_____

Filing cabinet

_____

_____

_____

Film

_____

_____

_____

_____

Fireworks

Flag

Flagpole

Flashlight

Flying saucer

Fork

Garbage

Gift

Glass

Glue

_____

_____

_____

Handwriting

_____

_____

_____

Hole

_____

_____

_____

Jack-o-lantern

_____

_____

_____

Jar

_____

_____

_____

Key

_____

_____

_____

Knife

_____

_____

_____

Knot

_____

_____

_____

Laundry

_____

_____

_____

_____

_____

Leather

_____
_____
_____

Letter

_____
_____
_____

License

_____
_____
_____

Light

_____
_____
_____

Light bulb

_____
_____
_____

Lock

_____
_____
_____

Luggage

_____
_____
_____

Magazine

_____
_____
_____

Manure

_____
_____
_____
_____

Medicine

_____

_____

Money

_____

_____

Mug

_____

_____

Ornament

_____

_____

Package

_____

_____

Paint

_____

_____

Painting

_____

_____

Paper

_____

_____

Paper clip

_____

_____

_____

Paper towel

Pen

Piggy bank

Pillow

Pipe

Radio

Safety pin

Scales

Smiley face

Stapler

_____

_____

_____

Tea/tea bag/tea pot

_____

_____

_____

Telephone

_____

_____

_____

Thread

_____

_____

_____

Throne

_____

_____

_____

Tissues

_____

_____

_____

Treasure

_____

_____

_____

Umbrella

_____

_____

_____

Vase

_____

_____

_____

_____

Water bottle

Cymbals
_____
_____
_____

Drum
_____
_____
_____

Flute
_____
_____
_____

Guitar
_____
_____
_____

Harp
_____
_____
_____

Horn
_____
_____
_____

Instrument
_____
_____
_____

Keyboard
_____
_____
_____

Piano
_____
_____
_____

Abacus

_____

_____

_____

Anchor

_____

_____

_____

Arrow

_____

_____

_____

Axe

_____

_____

_____

Binoculars

_____

_____

_____

Blueprint

_____

_____

_____

Chain

_____

_____

_____

Clamp

_____

_____

_____

Clay

_____

_____

_____

Compass

_____

_____

_____

Cooking spoon

_____

_____

Crutch

_____

_____

Engine

_____

_____

Eraser

_____

_____

Fishing rod

_____

_____

Gun

_____

_____

Hammer

_____

_____

Handcuffs

_____

_____

_____

_____

_____

Hoe

_____

_____

_____

Hurdle

_____

_____

Ink

_____

_____

Knitting needles

_____

_____

Ladder

_____

_____

Lance

_____

_____

Life jacket

_____

_____

Machine

_____

_____

Magnet

_____

_____

_____

_____

Magnifying glass

_____

_____

_____

Microphone

_____

_____

_____

Microscope

_____

_____

_____

Nail

_____

_____

_____

Needle

_____

_____

_____

Net

_____

_____

_____

Noose

_____

_____

_____

Oar

_____

_____

_____

Paddle

_____

_____

_____

_____

Parachute

Pen

Pencil

Pin cushion

Poison

Rocket

Rope

Saw

Shovel

Staff

_____

_____

_____

Sword

_____

_____

_____

Torch

_____

_____

_____

Wand

_____

_____

_____

Wrench

_____

_____

_____

_____

_____

_____

_____

_____

_____

_____

_____

_____

_____

_____

_____

_____

_____

_____

Objects - Toys and games

Ball

_____

_____

_____

Balloon

_____

_____

_____

Board game

_____

_____

_____

Cards

_____

_____

_____

Cards: Clubs

_____

_____

_____

Cards: Diamonds

_____

_____

_____

Cards: Hearts

_____

_____

_____

Cards: Spades

_____

_____

_____

Computer game

_____

_____

_____

Darts

Dice

Doll

Doll house

Football

Jungle gym

Kite

Puppet

Rocking horse

Scooter

_____

_____

_____

Slide

_____

_____

_____

Swing

_____

_____

_____

Teddy bear

_____

_____

_____

Trampoline

_____

_____

_____

_____

_____

_____

_____

_____

_____

_____

_____

_____

_____

_____

_____

_____

_____

People

Ancestors
_____
_____
_____

Audience
_____
_____
_____

Baby

_____

_____

_____

Boy

_____

_____

_____

Child

_____

_____

_____

Choir

_____

_____

_____

Dwarf

_____

_____

_____

Elderly man

_____

_____

_____

Elderly woman

_____

_____

_____

Family

_____

_____

_____

Father

_____

_____

_____

_____

_____

Gang

Girl

Gypsy

Jury

Man

Mother

Orchestra

Parade

Party

Person

_____

_____

_____

Speaker

_____

_____

_____

Teenager

_____

_____

_____

Toddler

_____

_____

_____

Virgin

_____

_____

_____

Woman

_____

_____

_____

_____

_____

_____

_____

_____

_____

_____

_____

_____

People - Activities

Applause

Biking

Burp(ing)

Chewing

Choking

Climbing

Cooking

Crafting

Dancing

Driving

_____
_____
_____

Drowning

_____
_____
_____

Fighting

_____
_____
_____

Flying

_____
_____
_____

Gardening

_____
_____
_____

Golf(ing)

_____
_____
_____

Juggling

_____
_____
_____

Jumping

_____
_____
_____

Kissing

_____
_____
_____
_____
_____

Knitting/crocheting

_____

_____

_____

Knocking

_____

_____

_____

Operation

_____

_____

_____

Painting

_____

_____

_____

Sleeping

_____

_____

_____

_____

_____

_____

_____

_____

_____

_____

_____

_____

_____

_____

_____

People – Clothing and accessories

Apron

Backpack

Bag

Bathing suit

Belt

Bra

Bracelet

Braided hair

Cane

People - Clothing and accessories

Cap

Coat

Costume

Cuff links

Earrings

Engagement ring

Fur

Glasses

Gloves

Graduation cap/gown

_____

_____

_____

Handkerchief

_____

_____

_____

Hat

_____

_____

_____

Helmet

_____

_____

_____

Jacket/coat

_____

_____

_____

Jeans

_____

_____

_____

Jewelry

_____

_____

_____

Kimono

_____

_____

_____

Necklace

_____

_____

_____

_____

_____

Pants

Parasol

Perfume/cologne

Pocket watch

Purse/handbag

Ring

Scarf

Shirt

Shoe(s)

Shorts

_____

_____

_____

Sock(s)

_____

_____

_____

Tattoo

_____

_____

_____

Tie

_____

_____

_____

Veil

_____

_____

_____

Wallet

_____

_____

_____

Watch

_____

_____

_____

_____

_____

_____

_____

_____

_____

_____

_____

Accident

_____

_____

_____

Battle

_____

_____

_____

Birth

_____

_____

_____

Death

_____

_____

_____

Divorce

_____

_____

_____

Funeral

_____

_____

_____

Marriage/wedding

_____

_____

_____

_____

_____

_____

_____

_____

_____

_____

People - Mythical

Alien

Genie

Ghost

Giant

Mermaid

People - Professions

Athlete

Butcher

Carpenter

Cheerleader

Conductor

Cook

Delivery person

Doctor

Firefighter

Gangster

Gladiator

Homeless person

Jockey

Judge

King

Knight

Magician

Maid

People - Professions

Mail carrier

Nurse

Pilot

Pirate

Plumber

Police

Prince

Princess

Queen

Wanderer

Places

Airport

Abbey

Amusement park

Arch

Apartment

Bank

Bridge

Church

Carnival

Carousel

Castle

_____

_____

_____

Cave

_____

_____

_____

Cemetery

_____

_____

_____

Circus

_____

_____

_____

City

_____

_____

_____

Dam

_____

_____

_____

Dungeon

_____

_____

_____

Elevator

_____

_____

_____

Emergency room

_____

_____

_____

_____

Factory

_____

_____

Finish line

_____

_____

Fountain

_____

_____

Garage

_____

_____

Grave

_____

_____

Grocery store

_____

_____

Gym

_____

_____

Harbor

_____

_____

Hospital

_____

_____

_____

_____

House

_____

_____

Igloo

_____

_____

Jail/prison

_____

_____

Jungle

_____

_____

Las Vegas

_____

_____

Library

_____

_____

Lighthouse

_____

_____

Mall

_____

_____

Merry-go-round

_____

_____

_____

_____

Monastery

Museum

Pedestal

Pier

Pillar

Playground

Restaurant

Roller coaster

Roulette wheel

School

Shop/store

Slot machine

Stage

Statue

Tomb

Tower

Well

Zoo

Places - Geographical Areas

Africa

Antarctica

Asia

Australia

Canada

Central America

China

Continent

Europe

France

_____

_____

_____

Germany

_____

_____

_____

Italy

_____

_____

_____

Japan

_____

_____

_____

North America

_____

_____

_____

South America

_____

_____

_____

USA

_____

_____

_____

_____

_____

_____

_____

_____

_____

_____

_____

Places - Landmarks

Arc de Triomphe

_____
_____
_____

Berlin Wall

_____
_____
_____

Big Ben

_____
_____
_____

Colosseum

_____
_____
_____

Eiffel Tower

_____
_____
_____

Empire State Building

_____
_____
_____

Fort Knox

_____
_____
_____

Golden Gate Bridge

_____
_____
_____

Great Wall of China

_____
_____
_____

Hollywood sign

Kilimanjaro

Leaning Tower of Pisa

London Eye

Mount Everest

Niagara Falls

Notre Dame

Pompeii

Pyramids of Giza

St. Peter's Basilica

_____

_____

Statue of Liberty

_____

_____

Stonehenge

_____

_____

Sydney Opera House

_____

_____

Taj Mahal

_____

_____

The Forbidden City

_____

_____

The Great Sphinx

_____

_____

Times Square

_____

_____

Tokyo Tower

_____

_____

_____

_____

Tower Bridge

Twin Towers

Versailles

Religious and Spiritual Symbols

Adam and Eve

_____

_____

_____

Akashic records

_____

_____

_____

_____

Altar

_____

_____

Angel

_____

_____

Arc

_____

_____

Ark

_____

_____

Aura

_____

_____

Bible

_____

_____

Bishop

_____

_____

Buddha

_____

_____

Buddha eyes

_____

_____

_____

_____

Religious and Spiritual Symbols

Celtic cross

_____

_____

Christmas lights

_____

_____

Christmas tree

_____

_____

Claddagh

_____

_____

Conch shell

_____

_____

Cross

_____

_____

Crucifix

_____

_____

Crystal ball

_____

_____

Dead body/bodies

_____

_____

_____

Devil

_____

_____

_____

Dove

_____

_____

_____

Egyptian ankh

_____

_____

_____

Endless knot

_____

_____

_____

Fish

_____

_____

_____

Gandhi

_____

_____

_____

Ganesh

_____

_____

_____

God

_____

_____

_____

Goddess

_____

_____

_____

_____

Religious and Spiritual Symbols

Golem

_____

_____

_____

Halo

_____

_____

Headless person

_____

_____

Hearse

_____

_____

Heaven

_____

_____

_____

Hell

_____

_____

Idol

_____

_____

_____

Jesus

_____

_____

Jesus/Christ

_____

_____

_____

_____

Kali

_____

_____

_____

Koran

_____

_____

_____

Lotus flower

_____

_____

_____

Madonna (Biblical)

_____

_____

_____

Mandala

_____

_____

_____

Nun

_____

_____

_____

Olive branch

_____

_____

_____

Peace sign

_____

_____

_____

Pendulum

_____

_____

_____

_____

_____

Pentagram/5-pointed star

_____

_____

_____

Praying hands

_____

_____

_____

Presents

_____

_____

_____

Priest

_____

_____

_____

Rosary

_____

_____

_____

Saint

_____

_____

_____

Scrolls

_____

_____

_____

Serpent

_____

_____

_____

Star of David/6-pointed star

_____

_____

_____

_____

Swastika

_____

_____

_____

Temple

_____

_____

_____

Third eye

_____

_____

_____

Vishnu

_____

_____

_____

Wheel

_____

_____

_____

Yin-Yang

_____

_____

_____

_____

_____

_____

_____

_____

_____

_____

_____

_____

_____

_____

_____

Shapes

Circle

_____

_____

_____

Cube

_____

_____

_____

Curve

_____

_____

_____

Cylinder

_____

_____

_____

Diamond

_____

_____

_____

Hexagon

_____

_____

_____

Line

_____

_____

_____

Octagon

_____

_____

_____

Oval

_____

_____

_____

Shapes

Pyramid

Square

Star

Triangle

Tarot Cards

A note about Tarot cards and symbolism: Tarot cards are included in this symbol dictionary workbook because of their connection to archetypal imagery and symbolism. While each card in a tarot deck has an explanation and description of what it means when it's drawn and placed in a spread, your own meanings may vary. Tarot cards can be a useful tool in tapping into your intuition if you are drawn to them.

Tarot Cards - Major arcana cards

Zero, The fool

_____
_____
_____

One, The magician

_____
_____
_____

Two, The high priestess

_____
_____
_____

Three, The empress

_____
_____
_____

Four, The emperor

_____
_____
_____

Five, The hierophant

_____
_____
_____

Six, The lovers

_____
_____
_____
_____
_____

Seven, The chariot

_____

_____

_____

Eight, Strength

_____

_____

_____

Nine, The hermit

_____

_____

_____

Ten, The wheel of fortune

_____

_____

_____

Eleven, Justice

_____

_____

_____

Twelve, The hanged man

_____

_____

_____

Thirteen, Death

_____

_____

_____

Fourteen, Temperance

_____

_____

_____

Fifteen, The devil

_____

_____

_____

Sixteen, The tower

_____

_____

Seventeen, The star

_____

_____

Eighteen, The moon

_____

_____

Nineteen, The sun

_____

_____

Twenty, Judgment

_____

_____

Twenty one, The world

_____

_____

_____

_____

_____

_____

_____

_____

_____

_____

_____

_____

_____

Ace

Two

Three

Four

Five

Six

Seven

Eight

Nine

Tarot Cards - Minor arcana cards - Cups

Ten

_____

_____

_____

Page/Princess/Daughter

_____

_____

_____

Knight/Prince

_____

_____

_____

Queen

_____

_____

_____

King

_____

_____

_____

_____

_____

_____

_____

_____

_____

_____

_____

_____

_____

_____

Tarot Cards - Minor arcana cards - Pentacles

Ace
_____
_____
_____

Two
_____
_____
_____

Three
_____
_____
_____

Four
_____
_____
_____

Five
_____
_____
_____

Six
_____
_____
_____

Seven
_____
_____
_____

Eight
_____
_____
_____

Nine
_____
_____
_____

Ten

_____

_____

_____

Page/Princess/Daughter

_____

_____

_____

Knight/Prince

_____

_____

_____

Queen

_____

_____

_____

King

_____

_____

_____

_____

_____

_____

_____

_____

_____

_____

_____

_____

_____

_____

_____

_____

_____

Tarot Cards - Minor arcana cards - Swords

Ace

_____

_____

_____

Two

_____

_____

_____

Three

_____

_____

_____

Four

_____

_____

_____

Five

_____

_____

_____

Six

_____

_____

_____

Seven

_____

_____

_____

Eight

_____

_____

_____

Nine

_____

_____

_____

Tarot Cards - Minor arcana cards - Swords

Ten

_____

_____

_____

Page/Princess/Daughter

_____

_____

_____

Knight/Prince

_____

_____

_____

Queen

_____

_____

_____

King

_____

_____

_____

_____

_____

_____

_____

_____

_____

_____

_____

_____

_____

_____

_____

_____

Tarot Cards - Minor arcana cards - Wands

Ace

_____

_____

_____

Two

_____

_____

_____

Three

_____

_____

_____

Four

_____

_____

_____

Five

_____

_____

_____

Six

_____

_____

_____

Seven

_____

_____

_____

Eight

_____

_____

_____

Nine

_____

_____

_____

Ten

_____
_____
_____

Page/Princess/Daughter

_____
_____
_____

Knight/Prince

_____
_____
_____

Queen

_____
_____
_____

King

_____
_____
_____
_____
_____
_____
_____
_____
_____
_____
_____
_____
_____
_____
_____
_____

Traffic Signs

Arrow

_____

_____

_____

Corner

_____

_____

_____

Crossroad

_____

_____

_____

Dead end

_____

_____

_____

Do not pass

_____

_____

_____

Exit

_____

_____

_____

Fork in the road

_____

_____

_____

Lane reduction

_____

_____

_____

_____

_____

_____

Traffic signs

Left turn only

Low-clearance

One way

Path

Pedestrian crossing

Railroad crossing

Right turn only

Road/Street

Roundabout

Side road

_____

_____

Signal ahead

_____

_____

Speed limit

_____

_____

Stop

_____

_____

Traffic lights

_____

_____

Two-way traffic ahead

_____

_____

Winding road

_____

_____

Wrong way

_____

_____

Yield

_____

_____

_____

_____

Traffic signs

Vehicles and transportation

Airplane

Vehicles and transportation

Ambulance

_____
_____
_____

Bicycle

_____
_____
_____

Boat

_____
_____
_____

Bulldozer

_____
_____
_____

Bus

_____
_____
_____

Car

_____
_____
_____

Checkered flag

_____
_____
_____

Headlights

_____
_____
_____

Helicopter

_____
_____
_____
_____

Hot air balloon

Jet

Motor

Motorbike

Moving van

Plane

Plow

School bus

Ship

Vehicles and transportation

Taxi

_____

_____

_____

Tractor

_____

_____

Train

_____

_____

Truck

_____

_____

Unicycle

_____

_____

Van

_____

_____

Wheel(s)

_____

_____

_____

_____

_____

_____

_____

_____

Zodiac signs

Aquarius
_____
_____
_____
_____

Aries
_____
_____
_____

Cancer

_____

_____

_____

Capricorn

_____

_____

_____

Gemini

_____

_____

_____

Leo

_____

_____

_____

Libra

_____

_____

_____

Pisces

_____

_____

_____

Sagittarius

_____

_____

_____

_____

_____

_____

Zodiac

Scorpio

_____
_____
_____
_____

Taurus

_____
_____
_____
_____

Virgo

_____
_____
_____
_____
_____
_____
_____
_____
_____
_____
_____
_____
_____
_____
_____
_____
_____
_____
_____
_____
_____

Acknowledgments and Resources

There are many people who were influential in the creation of this workbook and without whose support it would not have come into being. One such group of folks are the mediumship development circle, who inspired and challenged me to create a symbol dictionary workbook for them to use. Special thanks go to Angel for proofreading.

The following books were invaluable in creating this workbook. You can use them to learn more about symbols, as well as look up the common or archetypal meanings of certain symbols (and then check what you read against your own intuition or gut feelings about what the symbol means to you).

Animal-Speak: The Spiritual & Magical Powers of Creatures Great and Small by Ted Andrews

The Book of Psychic Symbols: interpreting intuitive messages by Melanie Barnum

Learn to See: An approach to your inner voice through symbols by Mary Jo McCabe

The Pretty Big Book of Symbols: A handy quick reference guide with keyword meanings for over 1400 psychic symbols, animals, plants, gemstones, everyday objects and more! by Clare McNaul

Index

Made in the USA
Coppell, TX
11 May 2024